D0722087

VELOCITY

THE WORLD OF
MIXED MARTIAL ARTS

STRIKING, GRAPPLING, AND GROUND FIGHTING

THE SKILLS BEHIND MIXED MARTIAL ARTS

BY JIM WHITING

Consultant:
Robert Rousseau
Martial Arts Guide, *About.com*
Senior Writer, *MMAFighting.com*

Capstone
press®

Mankato, Minnesota

Velocity is published by Capstone Press,
151 Good Counsel Drive, P.O. Box 669, Mankato, Minnesota 56002.
www.capstonepress.com

Books published by Capstone Press are manufactured with paper containing at least 10 percent post-consumer waste.

Library of Congress Cataloging-in-Publication Data
Whiting, Jim, 1943–
    Striking, grappling, and ground fighting: the skills behind mixed martial arts / by Jim Whiting.
        p. cm. — (Velocity — the world of mixed martial arts)
    Includes bibliographical references and index.
    Summary: "Discusses the training and techniques of mixed martial arts fighters as well as highlights of well-known matches" — Provided by publisher.
    ISBN 978-1-4296-3425-0 (library binding)
    1. Mixed martial arts — Juvenile literature. I. Title. II. Series.
GV1102.7.M59W58 2010
796.8 — dc22   2009007337

Editorial Credits
Abby Czeskleba, editor; Kyle Grenz, designer; Eric Gohl, media researcher

Photo Credits
Corbis/Reuters/Kim Kyung-Hoon, 45; Corbis/Sygma/Evan Hurd, 38; Digital Vision, 4–5; Getty Images Inc./Jon Kopaloff, 12–13, 20, 26–27; Getty Images Inc./Markus Boes, 39; Getty Images Inc./Tasos Katopodis, 24; Getty Images Inc./WireImage/Ed Mulholland, 14–15, 18–19, 34–35; Getty Images Inc./WireImage/Gregg DeGuire, 30–31; Getty Images Inc./WireImage/Ryan Born, 22–23; iStockphoto/Gerville Hall, cover; iStockphoto/snowkoala, 33, 36–37; Newscom/Cal Sport Media/Louis Lopez, 40–41, 42, 43; Newscom/CSM/Josh Thompson, 16–17, 28–29; Newscom/Icon SMI/John Pyle, 32; Shutterstock/Aleksandar Todorovic, 10–11; Shutterstock/Jan de Wild, 8 (hammer); Shutterstock/keellla (chain link, throughout); Shutterstock/Michael Svoboda, 6; Shutterstock/Orange Line Media, 8–9; Wikimedia/United States Marine Corps/Cpl. Giovanni Lobello, 7

TABLE OF CONTENTS

PREPARING TO FIGHT

Long before a mixed martial arts (MMA) fighter takes on an opponent, he works hard to prepare for the match. MMA combines the powerful blows of boxing with the strikes and high-flying kicks of martial arts like kickboxing and karate. MMA also uses grappling moves from wrestling as well as ground fighting skills from martial arts like Brazilian Jiu-Jitsu (BJJ).

MMA fighters develop their own styles of fighting from these different sports and martial arts. These fighters train for hours in hopes of one day becoming the best MMA fighter the sport has ever known.

TRAINING

It used to be that a 300-pound (136-kilogram) fighter could easily defeat a smaller opponent without much effort. But that's hardly the case in today's MMA world. For this reason, fighters have to be in top physical condition if they want to stand a chance at winning a match.

GETTING PHYSICAL

MMA fighters train hard before they enter the eight-sided cage better known as the Octagon. To prepare for matches, fighters focus on physical fitness and endurance during workouts.

WAYS FIGHTERS DEVELOP ENDURANCE:

- running up steep hills

- using a harness to pull a sled full of weights

- running with a parachute (the open parachute creates resistance)

- swimming

- striking or grappling with another fighter

endurance — the ability to handle long periods of exercise

7

BUILDING STRENGTH AND POWER

Fighters lift weights to develop strength and power. Bodybuilders do a small number of **repetitions**, or reps, with heavy weights. MMA fighters do a large number of reps with lighter weights. This type of workout keeps their muscles working for long periods of time.

OTHER WAYS TO DEVELOP STRENGTH:

○ flipping tractor tires

○ swinging sledgehammers

○ carrying sandbags

repetition — the act of raising and lowering a weight during weight training

Fighters do more than just build endurance and strength. Trainers also help fighters develop a "game plan" against opponents. A fighter watches videos of his opponent's fights to study the moves the opponent may use. Fighters spend time picturing themselves beating an opponent to increase their self-confidence.

For MMA fighters, working out is their job — and it's not an easy one either. It's common for MMA fighters to train for five to six hours a day, close to 40 hours each week. Compare that to other athletes who end their workouts after only a few hours at the gym.

COUNTDOWN TO COMPETITION

Training for a fight involves more than just exercise. Because fighters burn so many calories during workouts, they often eat six or seven meals a day. A fighter may **dehydrate** himself a day before the weigh-in. Fighters may spend time in a sauna to sweat off pounds or hit the gym extra hard in hopes of making weight.

After the weigh-in, fighters slowly begin to drink more water and continue their normal eating habits.

WEIGHT CLASSES

FLYWEIGHT
125 lb (56.6 kg)
and lighter

BANTAMWEIGHT
125.1-135 lb
(56.7-61.2 kg)

FEATHERWEIGHT
135.1-145 lb
(61.3-65.7 kg)

* LIGHTWEIGHT
145.1-155 lb
(65.8-70.3 kg)

* WELTERWEIGHT
155.1-170 lb
(70.4-77.1 kg)

* MIDDLEWEIGHT
170.1-185 lb
(77.2-83.9 kg)

* LIGHT HEAVYWEIGHT
185.1-205 lb
(84-92.9 kg)

* HEAVYWEIGHT
205.1-265 lb
(93-120.2 kg)

SUPER HEAVYWEIGHT
265.1 lb (120.3 kg)
and heavier

* weight classes used by the UFC
All weight classes are current as of June 2008.

But why do fighters lose weight just to gain it back? Fighters train hard with the goal of being the strongest and heaviest competitor in a weight class. If a fighter loses enough weight, he can be bumped down a weight class. After the weigh-in, he gains weight by building muscle. This is why some fighters look heavier on the night of a fight than they did at the weigh-in just a few days earlier.

By this time, a fighter has spent countless hours training for the fight of his life. He's now ready to put his skills to the test against an opponent.

ON THEIR FEET

Excitement fills the air as an MMA fight begins. Thousands of cheering fans watch as two fighters get ready to settle the score inside the cage. A fighter uses striking, grappling, and ground fighting skills to punish an opponent. Matches begin with both fighters circling each other before closing in to attack.

Most fighters start a match using their striking skills. Fighters land blows with their fists, elbows, knees, and feet. Fans love to see high-flying kicks and hard-hitting blows.

Fighters must wait for the right time to attack. Otherwise, the match can end in a matter of seconds.

When Kimbo Slice took on Seth Petruzelli in a 2008 Elite XC matchup, fans expected Slice to win the fight. But when Slice threw the first punch of the match, it was met with a high kick from Petruzelli. A few more punches from Petruzelli sent Slice to the mat. Petruzelli threw punch after punch until the referee stopped the action. The match had ended less than 15 seconds after it had begun.

Fighters usually begin punching or kicking while in a standard **stance**. Fighters bend their knees slightly in this stance.

Fighters turn their bodies so that one side is facing the opponent. This position helps fighters keep their balance. Right-handed fighters stand with their left side facing an opponent. Left-handed fighters stand with their right side facing the opponent.

stance — the position of a fighter's feet and body

THROWING PUNCHES

Fighters use their hands to protect their faces. They also tuck in their elbows to protect their bodies. Once an attack begins, fighters use a combination of punches.

#1: THE JAB

The jab is the most commonly used punch. The jab can set up a **knockout**, but fighters often use the jab to defend themselves. Jabs keep an opponent from getting too close and launching an attack of his own. To throw a jab, a right-handed fighter steps forward with his left leg. He also shoots his left fist straight out. A left-handed fighter does the opposite.

knockout — a victory in which a fighter's opponent is unable to get up after being knocked to the ground

#2: THE CROSS

The cross is a great follow-up punch to the jab. A fighter throws a jab with his lead fist. He follows up the attack with a cross using his other fist. The opponent may be expecting the jab, but the cross is the real shocker. The fighter turns his hips and shifts his weight to the ball of his rear foot. At the same time, he throws his arm straight out. The punch crosses the fighter's body because he turns his hips. Fighters usually strike opponents in the head with a cross. The cross can do serious damage.

#3: THE OVERHAND

A fighter throws an overhand punch by turning his hips. Moving the hips causes one shoulder to move forward while the other moves backward. The fighter's fist quickly moves upward and then downward in a looping motion.

FACT: The overhand is sometimes called the overhand right or the go-to punch.

#4: THE HOOK

To throw a hook, the fighter bends his right arm at a 90-degree angle and turns his hips. When he turns off his front foot, his fist moves in a circular direction toward the opponent. A hook can be hard to block because of its curving path.

To knock out an opponent, a fighter throws hooks at his chin. To weaken an opponent, a fighter aims hooks at the body.

PUNCHING COMBINATIONS

Fans love to see a single punch end a fight in a heartbeat. But it usually takes a combination of punches to weaken an opponent.

Most combinations begin with a jab followed by another punch like the cross. A fighter can quickly deliver the cross after jolting the opponent with a jab.

Another combination is the jab-cross-hook. Just as a jab sets up a cross, a cross sets up a hook because the fighter switches arms to throw each punch.

#5: THE UPPERCUT

A fighter throws an uppercut when standing close to his opponent. The punch begins at waist level and targets an opponent's chin.

The fighter pushes forward and up off his leg. He also moves his hips and drives his fist upward at a 90-degree angle.

THE COUNTERPUNCH

Fighters use counterpunches to defend themselves against an opponent's strikes. A fighter can throw a counterpunch whenever his opponent throws a punch. If an opponent leaves his head or body unprotected when throwing a punch, a fighter targets the unprotected areas with a counterpunch.

FACT: The cross is a common counterpunch to an opponent's jab.

To counterpunch, a fighter waits for his opponent to throw a punch. The fighter then quickly moves his head to avoid his opponent's blow and throws a punch of his own. A good counterpuncher protects himself and tries to hurt his opponent every time he launches an attack.

If a powerful punch is thrown at just the right time, the fight may end with a knockout. But more often, both fighters remain on their feet.

19

LOCKED TOGETHER

If a fighter's strikes don't weaken his opponent, the two men may grapple with each other. Grappling begins with both fighters wrapping their arms around each other. This move is known as a clinch.

Clinches can happen at any point during the match. Fighters may move in and out of a clinch as the fight continues.

Fighters may keep striking an opponent during the clinch. Fighters deliver short punches, elbow strikes, and knee strikes to the opponent's midsection. These blows weaken an opponent.

FACT: Fighters can easily grip opponents because MMA gloves don't cover the fingertips.

DIRTY BOXING

Fighters can gain an advantage during a clinch by using "dirty boxing" moves. These moves can be used in MMA, but are against the rules in boxing. During a common "dirty boxing" move, a fighter grabs the back of his opponent's head and pulls it down. The fighter then uses his other hand to bash his opponent's face with a series of uppercuts.

A fighter can also put both hands on the back of the opponent's head to gain more control. A fighter pulls the opponent's head down. The fighter finishes by driving a knee into his opponent's face.

21

USING THE CLINCH

During a clinch, a fighter may trap his opponent against the chain-link fence to gain control. A trapped fighter can have difficulty using his legs. Fighters can also stomp on a trapped opponent's foot. If a fighter is getting pounded, he often moves into a clinch. The clinch lessens the power of his opponent's blows.

Ultimate Fighting Championship (UFC) fighter Randy Couture has a strong clinch thanks to his background in Greco-Roman wrestling. Greco-Roman wrestlers rely on upper-body strength because they can't use holds below the waist.

The clinch can also be used to set up a **takedown**. To take down an opponent, a fighter knocks the other man off balance. A fighter drops his hips and keeps his back straight to lower his **center of gravity**. The fighter must be careful not to lose his balance when he bends over.

FACT: UFC fighters Matt Hughes and Joe Stevenson are known for their takedowns.

takedown — an action in which a fighter forces an opponent to the ground

center of gravity — the point at which a person or object can balance

TYPES OF TAKEDOWNS

Takedowns may look different, but they all have one goal: to knock an opponent off his feet. Single-leg and double-leg takedowns are two of the most popular takedowns seen inside the Octagon.

To execute a takedown, a fighter drives his opponent to the mat. A fighter uses his body weight or shoulder to knock his opponent off balance. The force of the landing stuns the opponent.

SINGLE-LEG

During a single-leg takedown, the fighter grabs an opponent's leg and forces him to the ground.

The opponent may avoid the takedown by hopping to the fence and leaning against it.

A fighter may **shoot** toward an opponent during a takedown attempt.

But if the shooting fighter misses his opponent, the fighter can lose his balance and fall. With the tables turned, the opponent can score a takedown.

AVOIDING A TAKEDOWN

To avoid an opponent's takedown, a fighter steps forward and puts one leg between his opponent's legs. At the same time, the fighter thrusts his hips forward and straightens his back. Then he locks his hands behind his opponent's back and pulls him forward. The fighter finishes by using his other foot to step behind his opponent and trip him.

shoot — to make a sudden move

DOUBLE-LEG

If a single-leg takedown doesn't work, a fighter may try a double-leg takedown. During this move, the fighter bends his knees and drops low. He then shoots off his front leg toward his opponent's midsection.

The fighter wraps his arms around the back of his opponent's thighs and lifts him off the ground. Grabbing both legs causes an opponent to lose his balance.

A powerful slam to the canvas finishes off the takedown. With the stunned opponent on his back, the top fighter takes the advantage.

CHAPTER 4

TO THE MAT

The ground game begins when two fighters hit the canvas. Fans love watching the fight move to the ground game in hopes that one fighter will end the match once and for all.

THE GROUND FIGHTER'S ADVANTAGE

A fighter on his back is not completely helpless against his opponent. The closed guard, open guard, and half guard are three positions a downed fighter uses during a match.

CLOSED GUARD

The downed fighter may move into the closed guard to control his opponent. With his opponent on top of him, a fighter wraps his legs around his opponent's back. He uses his arms and legs to keep the top fighter from switching positions. The bottom fighter can try to change positions so that he's on top of his opponent.

OPEN GUARD

The downed fighter may move from the closed guard to the open guard. When a fighter moves from one position to the other, he unlocks his legs from around his opponent's back. During the open guard, the downed fighter may put one or both of his feet on his opponent's hips. The downed fighter can then use his hands to hold the opponent's wrist.

FACT: The closed guard is the most common ground fighting position.

Moving from the closed guard to the open guard increases the distance between the downed fighter and his opponent.

HALF GUARD

During the half guard, the downed fighter wraps both of his legs around one of his opponent's legs.

29

HELIO GRACIE

Helio Gracie was born on October 1, 1913. As a boy, he was too weak to practice jiu-jitsu with his brothers. He had no choice but to sit and watch. Helio became a little stronger when he was a teenager. He wanted to become a fighter even though he was small for his age. But he couldn't keep up with bigger opponents.

Helio developed a new style of fighting. His arms were too weak for regular jiu-jitsu. A fighter on his back normally was at a disadvantage. But Helio was able to control his opponents with his legs while in this position. When he applied chokeholds, he gave his opponents no choice but to give up. Helio's style of fighting was called Brazilian Jiu-Jitsu.

At 17, Helio began his professional fight career. Because he was willing to take on anyone, many Brazilians considered him the toughest man on earth.

Helio's final fight came in 1955 against his former student Valdemar Santana. The match lasted nearly four hours. Though Helio lost the fight, fans admired him for his endurance. Today people still remember his amazing contribution to the martial arts world.

THE GUILLOTINE

If the bottom fighter wants to quickly end the match, he goes for a chokehold like the guillotine. During this chokehold, the bottom fighter sits up, hooks one arm around his opponent's neck, and brings his hands together.

FACT: A fighter can perform a guillotine on his back or while standing.

A fighter can also perform a guillotine while in the closed guard. This position puts pressure on the top fighter's neck and hips because the bottom fighter's legs are wrapped around his waist. The closed guard also causes more strain on the top fighter's neck.

While it's possible to escape the guillotine, most fighters **tap out** before too long. The bottom fighter wraps his arm completely around his opponent's neck. The top fighter's air supply gets cut off during the guillotine. The top fighter may become unconscious if he waits too long to tap out.

tap out — to quickly hit something with one hand several times to signal defeat

THE TOP FIGHTER
TAKES CONTROL

If the top fighter avoids his opponent's guillotine, he can try to "pass guard" by freeing himself from his opponent's legs. A top fighter gains control of the match after passing guard.

To escape the closed guard, the top fighter may pin his opponent's wrists to the mat. The top fighter then begins to stand up. As he stands, the bottom fighter is forced to loosen his legs. The top fighter can also punch his opponent while trying to stand up.

The top fighter keeps most of his body weight on his opponent's chest. Then he shifts position so that he is on one side of his opponent. This move opens up the chance for a **submission hold**. He can also hook one arm under his opponent's shoulder and begin pounding him with his other fist.

COMMON FIGHTING STYLES

1. The *sprawl and brawl* style is a favorite style for fighters with a boxing or kickboxing background. When an opponent comes at him, a fighter locks his hips and slides his feet backward. The fighter moves his legs away from his opponent's reach and pushes down on his opponent's shoulders. This move leaves the opponent facedown and keeps him from scoring a takedown.

2. Fighters with a wrestling background commonly use the *ground and pound* style. A fighter takes down his opponent and gains control. The fighter then punches him until he is knocked out or taps out.

3. In the *lay and pray* style, a fighter has control of his opponent on the ground but can't win the match. It seems the fighter is stalling for time and "praying" for something to happen.

submission hold — a chokehold, joint hold, or compression lock that causes a fighter's opponent to end the match by tapping out or saying, "I submit."

The top fighter can use his fists or elbows to strike an opponent. But he has to make sure the blows are causing some damage. If the fighters reach a **stalemate**, the referee may halt the action and force both fighters to stand up.

The top fighter **mounts** his opponent to gain control. Mounting allows a fighter to strike his opponent over and over. The mount is one of the most powerful positions in MMA.

stalemate — a situation in which neither fighter has an advantage and no progress is being made in the match

The bottom fighter's only hope is that the mounted fighter loses his balance. The bottom fighter doesn't have many choices to defend himself. His best bet is to escape the mount by moving into a position like the guard. He may use his arms to block the mounted fighter's punches. But it's difficult for the bottom fighter to strike his opponent during a mount. If the bottom fighter turns to avoid his opponent's strikes, the mounted fighter can use a chokehold to end the match.

mount — to sit on top of an opponent and straddle his chest

SUBMISSION HOLDS

Either fighter can end the match if he waits for the right opportunity. The fight can be won by submission if the opponent taps out or screams, "I give up!" Fighters use three types of submissions to end matches: chokeholds, joint locks, and compression locks.

#1 CHOKEHOLD

During chokeholds, a fighter wraps his arms or legs around the opponent's neck. This move puts pressure on the opponent's windpipe and forces him to gasp for air. Chokeholds also cut off the blood supply to the brain.

#2 JOINT LOCK

In joint locks, a fighter puts pressure on the opponent's elbow, ankle, or other joint. A fighter also **overextends** an opponent's joint. The pain becomes so bad that the opponent can't continue.

The armbar is a common joint lock. During this move, a fighter wraps his legs around an opponent's arm. Not only does the armbar put pressure on the arm, but it also strains the elbow.

#3 COMPRESSION LOCK

During compression locks, fighters press an opponent's muscle or tendon against a bone. Two common compression locks include the bicep slicer and leg slicer. With the leg slicer, a fighter can put pressure on his opponent's thigh or calf muscle.

overextend — to stretch or straighten something past the level of comfort

FAMOUS FIGHT HIGHLIGHTS

The history of MMA is full of exciting fights. Here are four well-known matches that highlight just a few ways to end a fight.

GRACIE vs SEVERN

Royce Gracie faced Dan Severn in the UFC 4 championship match. Severn weighed nearly 100 pounds (45 kilograms) more than Gracie. But Gracie had won two of the first three UFC tournaments.

After sparring early in the match, Severn flung Gracie to the mat. Gracie took the closed guard position and wrapped his legs around Severn's back. Gracie seemed to be at a serious disadvantage as Severn pounded him for nearly 15 minutes.

When Severn changed position, Gracie quickly slid his hips out and shifted his legs high on Severn's back. Gracie used his legs to execute a triangle hold. As a result, Severn had no choice but to tap out.

Severn

UFC 4:

Gracie vs. Severn
December 16, 1994

Location:
Tulsa, Oklahoma

Match ended:
**15 mins., 49 secs.
into Round 1
Win by submission**

THE HISTORY OF THE UFC

Long before UFC started, Helio Gracie created Brazilian Jiu-Jitsu. The martial art showed that a small man could defeat a much larger opponent. Brazilian Jiu-Jitsu had no time limits, no referees, and few rules.

Starting in the 1980s, the Gracie family tried to bring the sport to the United States. The Gracies found Semaphore Entertainment Group (SEG), a company that was willing to work with them. SEG put on the first UFC tournament, UFC 1, on November 12, 1993. Eight men competed at UFC 1. Royce Gracie won the UFC 1 championship.

SEG sold the UFC to Zuffa in 2001. Zuffa is run by UFC president Dana White, along with Lorenzo Fertitta and Frank Fertitta III.

FACT: Royce Gracie competed in three matches at UFC 1. Gracie beat Art Jimmerson in less than three minutes. This match was Gracie's longest fight of the night.

39

HUGHES vs PENN

UFC 63 wasn't the first time Matt Hughes and B.J. Penn had met inside the Octagon. Their first match came on January 31, 2004, at UFC 46. Penn used a submission hold in the first round to defeat Hughes and win the welterweight title. When Penn left the UFC in 2004, he was stripped of his title.

Hughes was the current welterweight champion leading up to the rematch. Hughes had won all five of his matches against other opponents before meeting Penn a second time. On the other hand, Penn had fought in just one UFC match since UFC 46. His loss came at the hands of Georges St-Pierre.

With the welterweight title on the line once again, it was clear these two fighters had a score to settle. The match began with both fighters circling each other before the first punch was thrown. Less than 30 seconds into the fight, Hughes went for a single-leg takedown in the middle of the Octagon. With one of Penn's legs in Hughes' grip, the two fighters moved against the fence. But Penn wouldn't allow Hughes to take him down.

Hughes' first successful takedown of the match came early in the second round. Penn used the closed guard as Hughes moved him against the fence. Hughes tried to stand and pass guard, but Penn used another closed guard to maintain control of his opponent.

With less than one minute left in the second round, Penn put Hughes in a triangle chokehold. Things didn't look good for Hughes. It seemed like only a matter of time before he would tap out. Surprisingly, Hughes survived the submission hold until the clock ran out. This match was turning out to be a fight for the record books.

Hughes started the third round with straight punches and combinations. As the round continued, Penn was clearly growing tired. It seemed the match was turning in Hughes' favor.

Hughes took his opponent to the mat and used nonstop punches to weaken Penn. The referee finally stopped the match and awarded Hughes the **technical knockout** (TKO).

UFC 63:

Hughes vs. Penn
September 23, 2006

Location:
Anaheim, California

Weight Class:
Welterweight
155.1–170 lb
(70.4–77.1 kg)

Match ended:
3 mins., 53 secs.
into Round 3
Win by TKO

technical knockout — the act of stopping a fight when a fighter is at risk of serious injury if the fight continues

LAUZON vs PULVER

Before meeting Jens Pulver at UFC 63, Joe Lauzon's MMA record included 13 wins and three losses. But Lauzon had only competed in other MMA organizations. This was his first time entering the Octagon. Pulver, a former UFC lightweight champion, left the UFC in 2002, but returned shortly before his UFC 63 match. Because Pulver had six wins, no losses, and one draw in the UFC, most people thought he would have an easy time finishing off Lauzon.

Pulver had a background in boxing and Lauzon knew better than to trade punches with him. After a few seconds of sparring, Lauzon took down Pulver,

Pulver escaped and tried to land a punch, but his feet weren't in the right position. He fell to his knees. Pulver was still off balance when he scrambled to his feet. Lauzon took advantage of Pulver's mistake. Lauzon drove a knee into Pulver's midsection and launched a punch that knocked Pulver on his back. Lauzon rained down hard blows. The referee ended the fight less than a minute after it began and awarded Lauzon the knockout.

Joe Lauzon sat on the Octagon's fence as he celebrated his win against Jens Pulver at UFC 63.

UFC 63:

Lauzon vs. Pulver
September 23, 2006

Location:
Anaheim, California

Weight Class:
Lightweight 145.1–155 lb (65.8–70.3 kg)

Match ended:
48 secs. into Round 1 Win by knockout

EMELIANENKO vs CHOI

Before his fight against Hong Man Choi, Fedor Emelianenko was known as the World's Best Heavyweight. On the other hand, Choi was known as the World's Biggest Heavyweight.

Emelianenko stood 6 feet (1.8 meters) tall and weighed a solid 235 pounds (107 kilograms). Choi was 7 feet, 2 inches (2.2 meters) tall and weighed 330 pounds (150 kilograms). Choi stood more than 1 foot (.3 meter) taller than his opponent. As if that weren't enough, Emelianenko had nearly a 100-pound (45-kilogram) disadvantage against his opponent. Choi was clearly living up to his name as the World's Biggest Heavyweight.

FACT: Emelianenko and Choi fought each other in a boxing ring.

Less than 10 seconds into the fight, Emelianenko tried to take down Choi. But Choi wrapped his arms around Emelianenko and fell on top of him. Emelianenko freed his legs and put Choi into the half guard. Emelianenko then moved to the closed guard.

When Choi changed his position, Emelianenko moved from the closed guard to an armbar. Emelianenko was upside down with his head and shoulders on the mat. Choi escaped by shaking off Emelianenko.

The two men scrambled to their feet. Emelianenko landed a blow and backed Choi into the ropes. Choi bounced off the ropes and fell on Emelianenko. Emelianenko again used the closed guard. When Choi raised his chest to strike harder, Emelianenko used another armbar. Choi tapped out less than two minutes into the fight.

Emelianenko vs. Choi
December 31, 2007

Location:
Saitama, Japan

Match ended:
**1 min., 54 secs.
into Round 1
Win by submission**

Jaw-breaking punches, exciting takedowns, and painful submission holds keep MMA fans on the edge of their seats. These moves, along with the talent of MMA stars, are why fans find the sport so entertaining.

45

GLOSSARY

center of gravity (SEN-tur UHV GRAV-uh-tee) — the point at which a person or object can balance

dehydrate (dee-HY-drayt) — to cause the body to lose a large amount of water

endurance (in-DUHR-uhnts) — the ability to handle long periods of exercise

knockout (NOK-out) — a victory in which a fighter's opponent is unable to get up after being knocked to the ground

mount (MOUNT) — to sit on top of an opponent and straddle his chest

overextend (oh-ver-ik-STEND) — to stretch or straighten something past the level of comfort; an MMA fighter overextends an opponent's joint during a joint lock.

repetition (rep-i-TISH-uhn) — the act of raising and lowering a weight during weight training

shoot (SHOOT) — to make a sudden move

stalemate (STAYL-mayt) — a situation in which neither fighter has an advantage and no progress is being made in the match

stance (STANS) — the position of a fighter's feet and body

submission hold (suhb-MISH-uhn HOHLD) — a chokehold, joint hold, or compression lock that causes a fighter's opponent to end the match by tapping out or saying, "I submit."

takedown (TAYK-doun) — an action in which a fighter forces an opponent to the ground

tap out (TAP OUT) — to quickly hit something with one hand several times to signal defeat

technical knockout (TEK-nuh-kuhl NOK-out) — the act of stopping a fight when a fighter is at risk of serious injury if the fight continues

unconscious (uhn-KON-shuhss) — not awake; not able to see, feel, or think.

read more

Franklin, Rich, and Jon F. Merz. *The Complete Idiot's Guide to Ultimate Fighting.* Indianapolis: Alpha, 2007.

Ollhoff, Jim. *Grappling.* The World of Martial Arts. Edina, Minn.: ABDO, 2008.

Ollhoff, Jim. *Martial Arts Around the Globe.* The World of Martial Arts. Edina, Minn.: ABDO, 2008.

Shamrock, Frank. *Mixed Martial Arts for Dummies.* Indianapolis: Wiley, 2009.

internet sites

FactHound offers a safe, fun way to find Internet sites related to this book. All of the sites on FactHound have been researched by our staff.

Here's all you do:

Visit *www.facthound.com*

FactHound will fetch the best sites for you!